D1562317

TREASURES

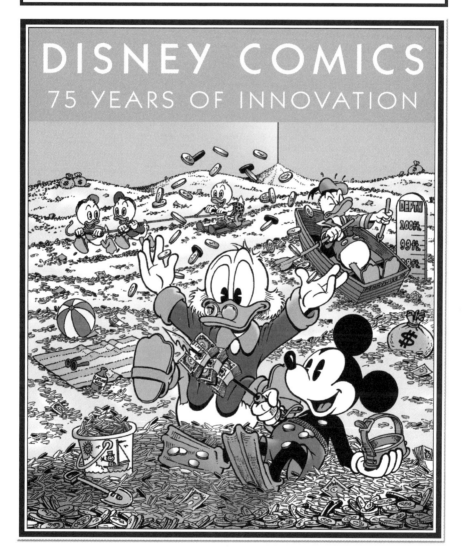

DISNEY COMICS
75 YEARS OF INNOVATION

THE OFFICIAL ANNIVERSARY BOOK

Stephen A. Geppi, *President/Publisher and Chief Executive Officer;* John K. Snyder Jr., *Chief Administrative Officer.* STAFF: Leonard (John) Clark, *Editor-in-Chief;* Sue Kolberg, *Assistant Editor;* Travis Seitler, *Art Director;* David Gerstein, *Archival Editor;* Melissa Bowersox, *Director-Creative Projects.* CONTRIBUTING STAFF: Gary Leach, Susan Daigle-Leach, *Art & Editorial.* ADVERTISING/MARKETING: J.C. Vaughn, *Executive Editor;* Brenda Busick, *Creative Director;* Jamie David, *Director of Marketing;* Sara Ortt, *Marketing Assistant, ads@gemstonepub.com;* Heather Winter, *Office Manager, Toll Free (888) 375-9800 Ext. 249;* Mark Huesman, *Production Assistant;* Mike Wilbur, *Shipping Manager;* Ralph Turner, *Accounting Manager;* Angie Meyer, Judy Goodwin, *Subscriptions, Toll Free (800) 322-7978.*

WALT DISNEY TREASURES
DISNEY COMICS: 75 YEARS OF INNOVATION

75 YEARS OF INNOVATION
by David Gerstein

Walt Disney often said that his cartoon empire "all started with a Mouse." But Disney animation existed before Mickey. It can also be argued that without the novelty of sound, the famed rodent would never have been an empire-starter. Now, to say that Disney's comic book empire started with a Mouse? That's more like it—there were no Disney comics before Mickey! Beginning with the Mouse and moving ahead, entire schools of creativity sprang up on multiple continents, hosting some of the medium's most creative innovators. So many greats have worked with Disney comics, in fact, that this—our official 75th anniversary book—can only begin to chronicle some of the exciting moments that our favorite mice, ducks, and dogs have experienced over the years.

Disney comics were born on January 13, 1930, with the launch of the Mickey Mouse daily newspaper strip. The strip's early gag stories, exemplified in this book by "Mickey Mouse Music" (1930), were soon supplanted by the adventure serials of Floyd Gottfredson, a master Mouse plotter with a unique take on Mickey's gang. The result, elaborate sagas like this book's "Foray to Mount Fishflake" (1934), were an international hit—and Mickey was an adventuresome, two-fisted international star. This led to the birth of a comic strip department within Disney—and the start of the *Silly Symphony* companion strip, in which artist Al Taliaferro refined the up-and-coming Donald Duck.

It also spawned a move into a new medium: Disney comic strips led to Disney comic books. In the 1930s, most such titles—exemplified by Western Publishing's *Mickey Mouse Magazine*—featured newspaper strip reprints. But some, like Britain's *Mickey Mouse Annual,* featured first-run comics production. Following the precedent set by the American newspaper strips, European Disney creators started out producing simple gag pages—like Wilfred Haughton's "Scoutmaster Mickey"—but quickly moved into longer-form sagas. By the end of the decade, English and Italian creators were writing and drawing the first long Donald Duck adventure stories.

The 1940s saw our domestic creators playing a masterful game of catch-up. As the "Golden Age" of American comics hit its stride, Western editor Eleanor Packer transformed *Mickey Mouse Magazine* into the 64-page *Walt Disney's Comics and Stories,* the first modern-style Disney comics title. Thicker than any previous periodical, *WDC&S* had room enough to reprint long Gottfredson Mickey epics one after another. But by 1942, Packer's newspaper strip backlog began to run low. If Western wanted more comics and stories, they would have to produce them themselves.

And so they did—putting the star power of Carl Barks, former Disney animation story man, behind Donald Duck. Like Gottfredson before him, "good Duck artist" Barks brought new subtleties to his funny animal hero; also like Gottfredson, Barks created an entire world of vibrant new supporting players. Two of the most famous, Gladstone Gander and Uncle Scrooge, are featured in this volume's "Race to the South Seas." Barks' creations proved that Disney comics stars could match the popularity of their on-screen relatives.

It was an emboldening realization for Western and for Disney's comic strip department, both of which hit their stride in the 1940s. Li'l Bad Wolf, Big Bad's goody-goody son, was created by editor Chase Craig, later meeting his definitive writer/artist in Gil Turner. Carl Buettner drew new tales of Bucky Bug, hero of Junkville town, while artist Paul Murry served up smart Brer Rabbit in memorable swampland sagas. And Pogo's Walt Kelly, drawing early *WDC&S* gags during World War II, told of crafty Gremlin Gus and his saboteur Widget pals.

Another kind of battle followed in the 1950s: the Cold War, in which Western society was marked by popular conservatism and a new contention that comics were for kids. But Disney comics survived these social changes. While never just for kids, Disney comics were always kid-*friendly.* And they could be conservative and progressive at once—by stocking a deceptively simple, traditionalist world with surprisingly three-dimensional, desire-driven characters.

At the time, these characters included farmer gal Grandma Duck, retooled from Taliaferro origins; the Beagle Boys, inimitable Carl Barks nogoodniks; Ellsworth, the cynical mynah bird; Chip 'n' Dale, the pesky chipmunks; and Pluto, whose stories were narrated by scripter Don Christensen in a delightfully tongue-in-cheek style. This book's "Chipmunk Monkeyshines" pairs dog, 'munks, Christensen, and Paul Murry, known in the 1950s for his Mickey Mouse tales.

Mickey himself endured a shake-up in the 1950s, when changes at Disney's comic strip department put an end to Gottfredson's adventure continuities. This was significant because these serials were still the mainstay of *Topolino,* Italy's powerhouse Disney weekly. Publisher Mondadori was forced to create its own replacement serials, bringing future comics legends Romano Scarpa and Giorgio Cavazzano to Mickey's world. As shown by this volume's Ellsworth tale, "AKA Cormorant Number Twelve," the new Italian creators preserved Gottfredson's take on the Mickey gang. But they also introduced great new characters—here, the no-good Trudy Van Tubb—and an increasingly modern and abstract artistic style.

The 1960s would see modernity bringing other changes to Disney comics. Over the first few years of the new decade, the American Disney magazines' circulation fell from 1,375,000 copies per issue to three hundred thousand. Disney publications director George Sherman blamed television and rival publishers, but another problem, quality slippage, might have also been to blame. Once aimed at all ages, Western Publishing's stories had begun to acquire the kids-only flavor of non-Disney humor comics.

Some creators made the best of this. The good side of childish storytelling, after all, is the creative whimsy you can mine by doing it right. In 1964, Western editor Chase Craig and writer Del Connell created Goofy's secret identity of Super Goof: arguably too silly to fit into the worlds of Barks and Gottfredson, but good satire still. The Disney studio, meanwhile, began producing its own comics for overseas use in 1962, and these too shared the new tone of wild whimsy. The "Studio program's" star characters included obsessive beatnik Fethry Duck and cynical tomcat Tabby; created by storyman Dick Kinney and featured here in "The Retriever," they remain leading lights of European Disney comics to this day.

Even as "Studio program" stories ran through the press, however, foreign creators were producing more and more Disney tales of their own. In Italy, an entire school of writers and artists followed Scarpa's and Cavazzano's lead. In Denmark, editor Knut Dokker arranged for Gutenberghus Publishing Service, today's Egmont Creative A/S, to begin producing its own Donald Duck material. In Brazil, publisher Abril carried on the tales of José Carioca, *Saludos Amigos'* (1943) dapper parrot star. And Dutch publisher Oberon, occasional producers of new material as early as 1954, now ramped up production significantly.

The 1970s saw a new element giving strength to these initiatives. Called "Donaldism," it was a burgeoning fandom for Disney comics' 1940s golden age, and it led professional fans to mimic Barks' and Gottfredson's early works. Dutch editor Daan Jippes and his colleagues—including Fred Milton and Thom Roep—created lovingly elaborate Donald comedies, such as this volume's "Sauce for the Duck." In Denmark, editors Lars Bergström and Stefan Printz-Påhlson encouraged the same trend among their own writers and artists—among them Marck Meul, Daniel Branca, and Victor Arriagada Rios (Vicar). Our "A Witch In Crime" exemplifies the works of the era.

Disney comics scholarship came to Italy and Brazil too in the 1970s. But these countries' comic creators were too busy riding their own inspirations to take in much outside influence. Brazil's Renato Canini carried José Carioca to new heights—and comedic lows—with a heavy dose of authentic Rio culture. And Italian creators were busy creating popular new characters. The superheroic Duck Avenger, created in 1969, hit his stride in the decade following, while the 1980s saw Bruno Sarda's creation of Arizona Dipp, Goofy's daredevil cousin.

The 1980s was also the decade when Donaldism came to America. Western's comic books had hit a low point; sold only in toy stores and featuring generally weak material, they sputtered out in 1984. But Disney fans with printing presses were active elsewhere. 1980 saw collectors Russ Cochran and Bruce Hamilton form the publishing house Another Rainbow. Initially the publishers of *The Fine Art of Walt Disney's Donald Duck*

(1980), a Carl Barks oil painting collection, and the famous *Carl Barks Library,* Another Rainbow followed on these successes by taking over the American Disney comic book license from Western.

With Byron Erickson as Editor-In-Chief, the new "Gladstone" comics imprint brought back Barks and Gottfredson, as well as giving European greats their first-ever exposure in English. But Erickson also produced first-run material, introducing the now-classic works of Don Rosa and William Van Horn. Rosa—represented in this book by his early "His Fortune on the Rocks"—sent Scrooge on numerous intricate treasure quests. "Loosey-goosey" William Van Horn took a different tack, drawing shorter and more comedic tales. Some, like the Gary Leach-written "Flights of Fancy," featured Launchpad McQuack, pilot star of the then-current *DuckTales* TV series.

DuckTales marked big changes at Disney. Revitalized by the early days of its Eisner and Katzenberg regime, it moved to exploit its comics properties as never before. Part of this plan, enacted in 1990, involved revoking Gladstone's license and publishing its own books in-house—which, while an ultimately unsuccessful effort, led to many new North American talents getting involved with ducks and mice. When Disney's plans imploded, these creators largely enlisted with Denmark's Egmont Creative A/S. The "Americans in Copenhagen" eventually included Don Rosa, William and Noel Van Horn, Janet and Michael T. Gilbert, Pat and Carol McGreal, John Lustig, Dave Rawson, and your present author, plus editors Byron Erickson (of Gladstone) and Bob Foster (of Disney).

This is not to say that Egmont, or any European publisher, has wanted for local creative talent in the 1990s or since. At Egmont, Lars Bergström, Stefan and Unn Printz-Påhlson, Henning Kure and other editors continue to produce "all-European" stories—including the notable work of writers Lars Jensen, Kari Korhonen, Gorm Transgaard, and Andreas Pihl. Modern-day Dutch stories—including the work of Jippes, writers Ruud Straatman and Frank Jonker, and artists Sander Gulien, Mau and Bas Heymans—have become internationally renowned. In Italy, finally, hyper-modern versions of Mickey, Duck Avenger, and the superheroic girls of *W. I. T. C. H.* have all enjoyed great success... though such non-traditional stories, great as they may be, lurk beyond the scope of this volume.

Here's to seventy-five years of Disney comics: seventy-five years of innovation, inspiration, and unforgettable creators. Legends like Carl Barks and Floyd Gottfredson have now passed on, but their heirs succeed the same way they succeeded—through simple respect for their readers and for their art form. Our comic stars may be talking animals, but our best works are not dumbed down; enslaved neither to the canard that kids require simplistic entertainment, nor to the superstition that older readers desire only easy self-parody. Artistic exploration and improvement have made the Disney magic for generations—and long may they continue to do so.

— *David Gerstein*

MICKEY MOUSE

in FORAY TO MOUNT FISHFLAKE

MICKEY MOUSE in

FORAY TO MOUNT
FISHFLAKE

 FORAY TO MOUNT FISHFLAKE

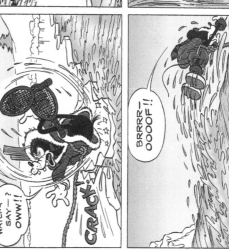

MICKEY MOUSE in FORAY TO MOUNT FISHFLAKE

14

MICKEY MOUSE

in

FORAY TO MOUNT FISHFLAKE

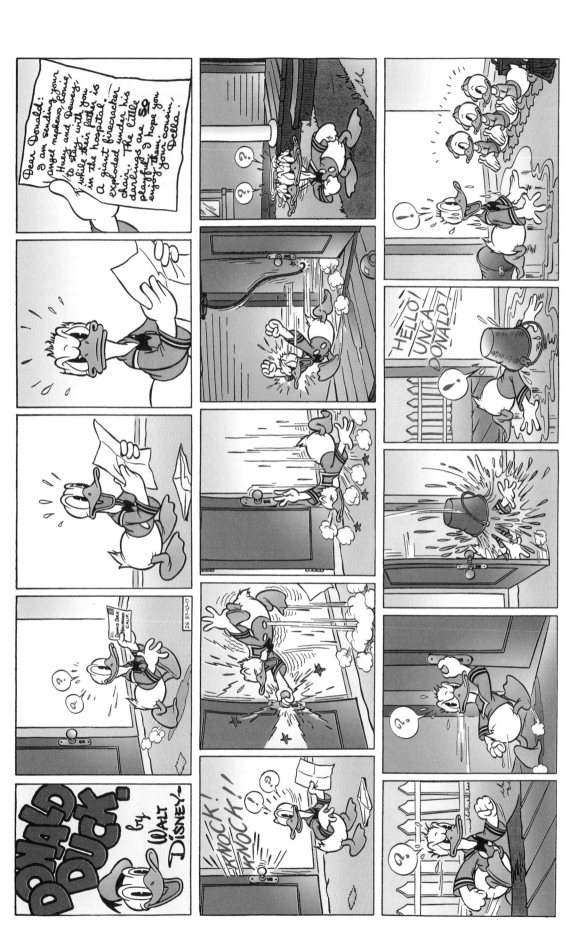

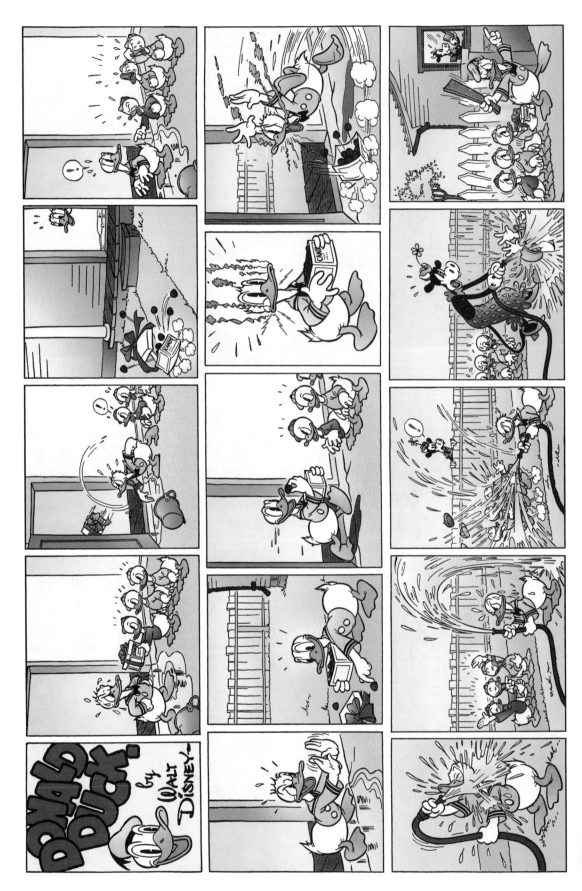

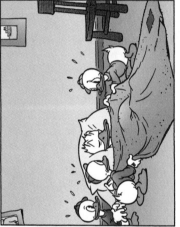

It's from your ma! she wants you to come back home!

RING!

? !

Oh! you don't, don'tcha?

Telegram for you, Unca Donald!

!

DONALD DUCK
by WALT DISNEY

WAAAAAAA! we want to stay here! we don't wanna go home!

W WDC 35-15

GREMLIN CUTOUT

"THE FIFINELLA"

WE'VE GOT A HELPER, GOOD AND STRONG, SO IT WON'T BE SO VERY LONG TILL WE SET SAIL IN OUR BALLOON TO FAR OSHKOSH OR SASKATOON!

THE BUGS BOTH WORK WITH MIGHT AND MAIN, UNTIL THE DAYLIGHT STARTS TO WANE....

AND THEN THEY WORK WITH MAIN AND MIGHT, THROUGH THE LONG HOURS OF THE NIGHT.

AT DAWN... THEIR HANDS ARE WORN AND CALLOUSED, BUT THEIR SHIP'S DONE ... AND HUNG WITH BALLAST.

AND NOW, KID, IF YOU'LL JUST STEP IN, OUR FLIGHT THROUGH CLOUDLAND WILL BEGIN!

THROW OFF THE BALLAST, SO WE'LL RISE!

YIPPEE!! WE'RE HEADED FOR THE SKIES!!

WE'RE HIGHER THAN I'VE EVER BEEN! HOW SOON'LL WE REACH GROUND AG'IN?

ULP! SOONER THAN YOU THINK, MY LAD....! OUR GOOD LUCK'S CHANGING INTO BAD!!

IN SOME WAY, BUCKY, WE'VE INCURRED THE WRATH OF THAT BIG, VICIOUS BIRD!!

IF SHE PECKS HOLES IN OUR BALLOON, WE'LL REACH THE GROUND, ALL RIGHT .... AND SOON!!

JOSÉ (JOE) CARIOCA by WALT DISNEY

SO THEES MOVIE STAR ARRIVING HERE AT THE AIRPORT EEZ AN OL' GORL FRAN', EH? WELL, I DON' BELIEVE EET!

WHAT WEEL I DO? HE'LL MAKE ME THE LAUGHING-STOCK OF RIO!

ALWAYS YOU TOL' OS FALLOWS WHAT A BEEG SHOTS YOU ARE! NOW I'LL FIND OUT FOR SURE!

WHAT'S THE MATTER, JOSÉ? YOU ACT NERVOUS, HEH!

I'VE GOT TO THEENK OF SOMETHEENG!

AH! I'LL BE RIGHT BACK!

TONI, THE OWNER OF LUCIA'S OPTOWN CAFE, EEZ GEEVING AWAY ALL THE GRAPE JUICE YOU CAN DREENK! HE'S A NEW PAPA!

HUH!

WOW! WHAT FON! WHAT TOO BAD YOU FALLOWS HAVE TO WORK...

SI? WHY?

PORTER'S STATION

FLIGHT FIVE NOW COMING IN AT GATE THREE.

THAT'S HER PLANE, JOSÉ!

SO EET EEZ!

OUT OF OUR WAY!

PORTERS STATION

ZIP ZIP

GULP! HE...HE'S WEETH HER!

HERE'S A TIP FOR CARRYING MY BAGS, SON, AND THANK YOU!

The End

MAX 25¢

COLLECT WALT DISNEY'S MOST TREASURED WORKS.

INTRODUCING 4 NEW WALT DISNEY TREASURES LIMITED SERIES VOLUMES.

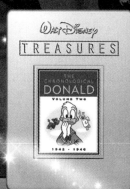

INDIVIDUALLY NUMBERED TWO-DISC SETS IN COLLECTIBLE TINS, EACH WITH AN EXCLUSIVE LITHOGRAPH.

NOW AVAILABLE ON Disney DVD

VISIT WALTDISNEYTREASURES.COM

A CLOSER LOOK AT
THE MONEY MINT AND *RACE TO THE SOUTH SEAS*
by David Gerstein

Disney comics have always been products of their time—but never more so than in their early days. Everything from the vintage stories' visual milieu to their cultural references bespoke prewar small-town America; or, more precisely, the way small-town America perceived itself, however divorced from reality such perceptions may have been. Characters' language reflected the era: a wallet was also called a "billfold" and shopping was "marketing." Expressions like "by gollies," "doggone it," and "for gosh sakes" were commonplace.

And then there was the Other: the way in which prewar pop culture represented those who came from groups outside America's white, semi-gentrified majority. Comics, films, and fiction at the time were all loaded with broadly caricatured, presumed humorous images of Africans, Asians, poor whites, Italians, and others "not like us," and Disney comics were not immune to the trend. For example, Disney characters from the Deep South—the allegorically African-American Brer Rabbit and white Brer Fox and Hard Haid Moe—spoke in thicker countrified dialect than they do today, while in Carl Barks' "Race to the South Seas," island natives were presented as primitives, some speaking educated English but others utilizing pidgin.

Before condemning these stories' creators, however, we need to take several factors into account. In comics' golden age, the use of ethnic and regional caricatures was not necessarily intended as hurtful. Stereotypes were seen by many as a natural element of humoristic shorthand—they were "what you used," as a creator of fiction, when you wanted to create quick laughs or add local color with minimal effort. So second-nature were these clichés, in fact, that the comics community's out-spoken supporters of civil rights—notably Walt Kelly and Theodor "Dr. Seuss" Geisel—could casually employ them, too, without pausing to think about their impact.

The exact nature of this impact, admittedly, is open to debate. A forward-thinking 1940s reader might have laughed at an eccentric, hayseedlike black character no differently than at a white hayseed—"they come in all colors," so to speak—and not let it affect his interactions with real-life African-Americans. Many minority audiences, too, took the era's negative stereotypes in stride. But it cannot be disputed that closed-minded individuals used negative stereotypes to bolster their prejudices, or that the general absence of positive stereotypes stood as a demoralizing factor for minorities.

This is not to say that Disney comics themselves were wanting for positive stereotypes. To their credit, Carl Barks, Floyd Gottfredson and others did try to strike blows for the oppressed, regardless of how minorities were otherwise portrayed. In "South Seas," for example, the island natives aren't dumb; some wise up to Gladstone's exploitation of them, while others' seeming fealty to Scrooge is revealed as a put-on for which they've been financially compensated. In Gottfredson's "Mickey Mouse Sails for Treasure Island" (not included in this volume), Mickey battles alongside a native tribe against explicitly white bad guys. And of course, Brer Rabbit forever outsmarts Brer Fox.

We hope you will look at "The Money Mint," "Race to the South Seas," and similar stories in *Walt Disney Treasures* as relics of their less enlightened time. We present the stories here in the interest of preserving their more enduring positive attributes for posterity—even if it means presenting history "warts and all."

— *David Gerstein*

Old-time Disney comics invoke ethnic and regional stereotypes—even as they mock Western culture for its faith in those stereotypes. In this example from "In Search of Jungle Treasure" (1937—not included in this volume), Goofy bears the brunt of the joke for his presumption that rural Africans should be uneducated.

BRER RABBIT DON'T AIM TO MARKET WID BRER FOX!

UH...UH!

BUT IT LOOKS LIKE SOMEBODY ELSE MARKETS IN MISTER MAN'S GARDEN, TOO!

TODAY...I LIKES CARROTS!

BRER RABBIT ALWAYS DOES HIS MARKETIN' IN MISTER MAN'S GARDEN...'CAUSE IT SAVES HIM A HEAP OF TRUBBLE...OR DOES IT?

Walt Disney Presents... "UNCLE REMUS" and his tales of BRER RABBIT Based on the stories by JOEL CHANDLER HARRIS

BUT NOBODY BUT A STUPID FOX WOULD CARRY A SACK WID A HOLE IN IT!

IMAGINE DAT STUPID FOX CARRYIN' CARROTS IN A SACK WID A HOLE IN IT.

ZB 46-02-24

DIS IS TOO EASY!

BRER RABBIT SEE RIGHT DAR DAT ALL HE'S GOT TO DO IS FOLLOW BRER FOX TO DO HIS MARKETIN'.

RABBIT STEW FER DINNER...RABBIT STEW FER DINNER...

I IS A NUMSKULL! I KNOWED ALL DE TIME DAT FOXES DON'T EAT CARROTS!

CONTINUED.

I GOT YOU! I GOT YOU, BRER RABBIT! I GOT YOU IN MY CARROT TRAP!

PO' BRER RABBIT DONE SLIPPED UP AGAIN!

BRER FOX IS SHO' A GEN'ROUS MAN!

SO BRER RABBIT FIGGER DAT FROM NOW ON HE'LL LET BRER FOX DO ALL HIS MARKETIN' FOR HIM!

35

THAT SAILBOAT IS YOURS, WITH MR. McDUCK'S REGARDS!

I-I CAN'T BELIEVE IT!

YOU MEAN HE-HE ACTUALLY GAVE ME THAT BOAT!

IT MUST BE A GAG! WHO ARE YOU, ANYWAY, MISTER?

SYLVESTER SHYSTER, MR. McDUCK'S PERSONAL LAWYER! I'LL READ HIS STATEMENT ABOUT THE GIFT!

"WHEREAS THE SAID GLADSTONE GANDER IS SO FULL OF WIND HE CAN SAIL A BOAT ON A STILL DAY, I AM PRESENTING HIM THIS TWENTY-FOOT SAILING CRAFT!

"MY REASON FOR MAKING THIS GIFT IS THAT UNDER CODE 6-A-77 OF THE TAX LAWS I CAN SAVE $3,876,943.85 IN INCOME TAXES! (SIGNED) SCROOGE McDUCK."

NOT VERY FLATTERING, BUT HE GAVE ME THE BOAT! WHAT WAS IT YOU SAID ABOUT YOU BEING HIS FAVORITE RELATIVE?

GRRR!

I'VE BEEN INSULTED! I'LL NEVER SPEAK TO UNCLE SCROOGE AGAIN—NEVER!

POOR UNCA' DONALD!

WAIT A MINUTE, YOUNG FELLOW! IF YOU'RE DONALD DUCK, I HAVE GOOD NEWS FOR YOU, TOO, FROM MR. McDUCK!

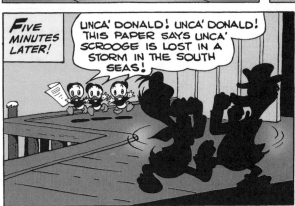

PREPARING FOR A LONG VOYAGE TAKES TIME AND MONEY! THE DUCKS GO ALL-OUT TO MAKE THEIR LITTLE BOAT READY FOR ITS BATTLE WITH THE STORMY SEAS!

HAVE WE GOT SALT BUTTER FOR OUR BREAD?

YES! HAVE WE GOT BREAD?

NO!

LOOK AT GLADSTONE! HE DOES NOTHING BUT SAIL AROUND THE BAY!

AND TALK BIG ABOUT RESCUING UNCA' SCROOGE!

SWELL! LET THE BIG SHOW-OFF HAVE HIS FUN! WE'LL BE HALFWAY TO THE SOUTH SEAS BEFORE HE GETS STARTED!

I WOULDN'T BE TOO SURE OF THAT! GLADSTONE WAS BORN LUCKY! HE DOESN'T HAVE TO LOAD HIS BOAT! SANTA CLAUS WILL DO THAT!

THAT EVENING!

WELL, EVERYTHING IS LOADED AND SHIPSHAPE! WE'LL ANCHOR IN OPEN WATER, SO AS TO BE READY TO SAIL WITH THE FIRST PUFF OF WIND!

FROM NOW ON I'M CAPTAIN, AND YOU'LL CALL ME 'SIR'!

AYE, AYE, SIR!

WE'RE READY TO SAIL, AND THERE'S GLADSTONE STILL TALKING BIG TO NEWSPAPER REPORTERS!

I DON'T LIKE IT!

LATER!

WHAT'S MAKING ALL THAT NOISE?

THE RACKET IS OVER BY THE DOCK!

IT'S A BUNCH OF MEN LOADING SUPPLIES INTO GLADSTONE'S BOAT!

AND GLADSTONE IS LOAFING ON TOP OF THE CABIN, PLAYING BIG SHOT AND TAKING IT EASY!

LISTEN! OUR RADIO—

GLADSTONE GANDER, COURAGEOUS NEPHEW-IN-LAW OF LOST TRILLIONAIRE SCROOGE McDUCK, SAILS AT DAWN FOR THE SOUTH SEAS TO RESCUE HIS RICH RELATIVE!

NOT A WORD ABOUT US!

TOUCHED BY GANDER'S HEROISM, LOCAL SHIP CHANDLERS ARE LOADING HIS TINY CRAFT WITH A COMPLETE STOCK OF FREE PROVISIONS!

UNCA' DONALD, YOU'RE TURNING PURPLE!

I KNEW IT! I KNEW IT! THAT GANDER GETS EVERY BREAK! HE'LL BEAT US TO UNCLE SCROOGE! WE HAVEN'T A CHANCE!

SIMMER DOWN, UNCA' DONALD! THE ISLANDS ARE A LONG WAY OFF!

ANYTHING CAN HAPPEN!

ANYTHING CAN HAPPEN TO US, BUT ONLY GOOD THINGS CAN HAPPEN TO HIM!

UNCA' DONALD IS LIKE A MADMAN!

I DON'T WONDER! GLADSTONE'S LUCK GETS TIRESOME AT TIMES!

SHALL I MAKE YOU A CUP OF TEA, UNCA' — SIR?

NO! SAVE IT! SAVE EVERY DROP OF WATER AND CAN OF BEANS!

IT'S 1500 MILES TO THE NEAREST ISLAND, AND WE CAN'T ROW MORE THAN A FEW MILES A DAY!

ULP!

DAY AFTER WEARY DAY!

ROW, ROW, ROW YOUR BOAT!

STOP THAT INFERNAL SINGING!

YEAH! TURN ON THE RADIO! MAYBE WE CAN PICK UP SOME CHEERFUL MUSIC!

GLADSTONE GANDER, HEROIC NEPHEW-IN-LAW OF LOST TRILLIONAIRE SCROOGE McDUCK, SAILED INTO COCA BOLA ISLAND HARBOR TODAY ON THE BACK OF AN OBLIGING WHALE!

CLICK! RRAAK!

HE HAS BROKEN ALL RECORDS FOR FAST OCEAN CROSSINGS, AND WHILE HELPFUL ISLANDERS REPAIR HIS STORM-BATTERED BOAT, HE INTENDS TO BASK IN THE TROPICAL SUN AND TAKE IT EASY!

NOT ONE WORD ABOUT US!

COME ON! COME ON, YOU SQUEALIN' SQUAWK BOX! SAY SOMETHING ABOUT US!

AND NOW SOME MUSIC! THE FOUR HEPCATS SINGING "HOW DEEP IS THE OCEAN?"

WITH HEAVY OARS AND LIGHT RATIONS, THE GLUM DUCKS ROW ON AND ON!

SHALL WE HAVE A BEAN FOR LUNCH, OR SKIP IT?

WE HAD A BEAN LAST THURSDAY! LET'S HAVE A PRUNE TODAY!

AT LAST THERE COMES A DAY!

LAND!

PALM TREES OFF THE PORT-SIDE!

ACCORDING TO THE CHARTS, THAT MUST BE COCA BOLA ISLAND!

WHERE GLADSTONE LANDED LONG LONG AGO!

MEANWHILE ON COCA BOLA GLADSTONE HAS BEEN LIVING ON THE FAT OF THE LAND!

BRING ME MORE ROAST PIGLET AND CANDIED YAMS!

AS OUR HONORED GUEST, OH GREAT ONE, YOUR EVERY WISH IS OUR COMMAND!

THAT GUEST EATS MUCH AND LINGERS LONG!

VERILY, HE WEARS THE WELCOME MAT THIN!

HIS BOAT HAS LONG BEEN READY TO SAIL, BUT STILL HE LIES IN THE SHADE AND EATS!

HE IS EVEN NOW EATING THE LAST OF OUR PIGLETS! WE FACE HUNGER BECAUSE OF HIM!

AS MAYOR, I MUST GO TO HIM AND STATE OUR CASE! AH, ME!

I COME, OH GREAT ONE, BEARING SAD TIDINGS!

SAVE 'EM! SAVE 'EM! WAIT TILL I EAT THESE VITTLES!

OKAY! IF WE HAVE TO CRACK THAT REEF THE HARD WAY, WE'LL DO IT! I'LL DYNAMITE A WAY THROUGH!

GRAB THIS FUSE LINE AND GET READY TO BACK OFF! THIS IS ONE CHANCE IN A THOUSAND!

BOOM

IT WORKED! THERE'S ROOM ENOUGH FOR THE BOAT AND A HALF-INCH TO SPARE!

NOW WE'RE EVEN AGAIN, GLADSTONE! MAY THE BEST MAN WIN!

MANY ISLANDS ARE SCANNED, THEN SUDDENLY—

UNCLE SCROOGE! I SEE UNCLE SCROOGE!

"IT'S HIM, ALL RIGHT! SPATS AND ALL! SITTING UNDER A TREE SIPPING A COCONUT!"

RUN THE BOAT ASHORE, BOYS, AND WE'LL GO GET HIM! HE'S NEAR THE TOP OF THAT FIRST RIDGE!

THOSE CANNIBALS WEREN'T CANNIBALS!

THEY'RE UNCLE SCROOGE'S HIRED STOOGES!

GLADSTONE GANDER! YOU—**YOU** HERE!

I CAME TO RESCUE YOU, UNCLE SCROOGE!

I CAN BET YOU WERE **GREATLY** WORRIED ABOUT ME! DID DONALD COME, TOO?

NO, UNCLE SCROOGE! I'M SORRY ABOUT DONALD! HE JUST DIDN'T SEEM TO CARE!

I **LIKE** THAT! AND AS FOR YOU, GLADSTONE, I'M **NOT** YOUR UNCLE, AND I DON'T **WANT** TO BE **RESCUED**!

BUT—YOUR PLANE CRASHED—AND—

I **HAD** THAT PLANE CRASHED! I DID IT SO I COULD COME TO THIS PREPARED HIDE-OUT AND RUN MY BUSINESS WITHOUT SEEING **ANY** OF MY **RELATIVES**!

ULP!

AND NOW **YOU** FIND ME—EVEN HERE! JUST FOR THAT, I'M CUTTING YOU OUT OF MY WILL!

I'LL LEAVE MY FORTUNE TO **DONALD DUCK**, WHO WAS KIND ENOUGH TO KEEP HIS LONG-NOSED FACE OUT OF MY SIGHT! NOW **GIT**!

HOW'S OLD **LUCKY** GLADSTONE, TONIGHT?

YEAH! HOW DO YOU FEEL?

GRRR!

U.S.A. ←

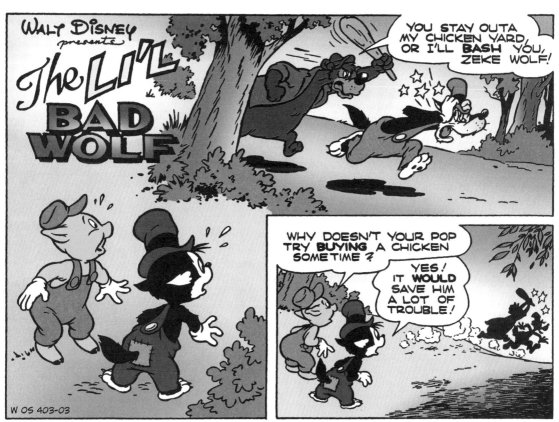

POP SENT ME TO SWIPE A CHICKEN... AND HE'LL EXPECT IT TO LOOK GOOD!

AND SO...

WHOOP-DE-DO! WHOOP! WHOOP! WHOOP!

HOT DOGGIES! LI'L WOLF SNITCHED A CHICKEN! THAT'S GOOD... 'CAUSE TH' CHICKEN BUYER IS WAITIN' AT MY BACK DOOR!

SLAM

I'M PROUD OF YOU, SON! YOU'VE REALLY GOT TH' KNACK! YOU'LL GROW UP TO BE A REAL BAD WOLF AFTER ALL!

YES, INDEEDY! NOW TO DELIVER IT TO MY BUYER AT TH' BACK DOOR...

TRA-LA-LA ♪ ♪

POP'S SO HAPPY THINKING I REALLY SWIPED IT, THERE'S NO POINT IN SPOILING HIS FUN!

TUM DE DUM ♪ DUM ♪ TUM ♪ TUM

THIS COULD TURN OUT TO BE A REAL GOOD THING!

I'D BETTER PUT THIS MONEY IN A SAFE SPOT... HM·M·M... TH' OL' SUGAR BOWL WOULD BE A PEACHY PLACE!

I'LL KEEP SENDIN' LI'L WOLF AFTER CHICKENS! HE MAY EVEN DEVELOP TH' HABIT HIMSELF!

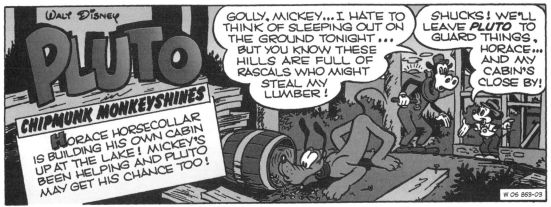

W OS 853-03

'COURSE, *CATCHING* FISH IS WONDERFUL SPORT! LISTEN HERE, GOOF— "CORMORANT FISHING CONTEST TODAY!"

WHUT KINDA FISHIN'?

CORMORANT FISHING! THEY'RE BIG, DOPEY BIRDS THAT *DIVE* TO CATCH FISH! AND YOU CAN *TRAIN* THEM TO CATCH 'EM *FOR* YOU!

HI, GOOFY! HOWDY, ELLSWORTH! HOME-COOKING, EH?

WHERE YUH HEADED, HORACE?

HEY, A *CORMORANT!* ENTERING THE CONTEST, PAL?

GOOD GUESS! AND MY *VICTORY'S* A FAIT ACCOMPLI!

I WOULDN'T BE SURPRISED! LOOKS LIKE HE'S GOT A KEEN EYE!

YEP! JUST LIKE *ME,* HE'S A FISHING CHAMP!

AND HAVE *WE* WON PRIZES? ∫HAW!∫ BY THE *BOATLOAD!* HE TIED FOR FIRST IN THE DUSTY LAKE FINALS! THEN WE WENT ON TO THE *REGIONALS* AT THUNDER BAY, AND AFTER *THAT* BLAH-BLAH YAKKETY-SHMACKETY...

I'LL TAKE CARE OF OUR GEAR, GOOFY! YOU JUST KEEP THE *PEDAL* TO THE METAL!

GOTCHA!

MOUSETON, THE CORMORANT HAS LANDED!

CORMORANT FISHING CONTEST

LOOKIT ALL THUH CONTESTANTS! AN' LOOKIT THUH *POLICE* BOATS OUT THERE, WATCHIN' OVER THINGS!

NUMBER 12? YOUR ROCK IS OVER THERE, SIR!

SAY! IS THERE *ALWAYS* THIS MUCH *SECURITY* AT CORMORANT FISHIN' CONTESTS?

≥HEH!≤ THOSE POLICE BOATS AREN'T FOR US! THE COPS THINK THERE'S SOME *JEWEL SMUGGLING* GOING ON AROUND HERE, SO THEY'RE KEEPING A CLOSE WATCH ON THE SHORELINE!

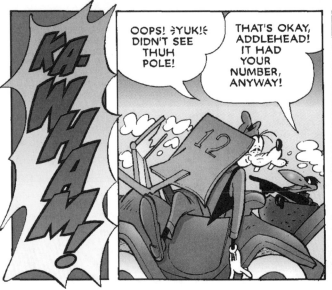

NOT BAD! I'VE PICKED UP THREE FISH FOR GOOFY AND TAUGHT THAT DINNER-SNATCHING GLUTTON A LESSON!

OOPS! *ANOTHER* CORMORANT! LOW BRIDGE, BUSTER!

HOLD THE PHONE! THAT WAS *TRUDY'S* BIRD! AND HE *DROPPED* SOMETHING SHINY!

A *DIAMOND* THE SIZE OF A *LEMON!*

HERE YOU GO, GOOFY! WILL THIS DO?

YOU *BET*, ELLSWORTH!

CONTESTANT NO. 10, HORACE HORSECOLLAR, HAS *WITHDRAWN* FROM THE CONTEST DUE TO *TECHNICAL DIFFICULTIES!*

GAWRSH! I'M REAL SORRY!

BUT NOW WE CAN LEAVE, TOO! I DON'T CARE ABOUT THUH PRIZE—I'VE GOT THUH FISH I NEED!

AWRIGHT, GOOF! GIVE ME JUST FIVE MORE MINUTES...

OH, AND A FRESH *OXYGEN* BOTTLE! I CRAVE ONE MORE PEEP IN THE DISMAL DEEP!

SWELL!

NOW *REMEMBER*, GOOFY...IF I GIVE *TWO TUGS* ON THE ROPE, PULL THE LINE IN SLOWLY AND HAUL ME UP! GOT IT?

RIGHTY-O, PAL!

HMM! TRUDY'S CORMORANT WENT FOR ANOTHER DIVE!

¿SNIFF!¿ THIS ONE'S *EMPTY!* THAT *BIRD-BRAIN!*

HERE'S WHERE I CONFIRM A *MAJOR* SUSPICION!

HE'S HEADED WAY OUT TO SEA! CHECK!

TWO PULLS! I'M READIN' YUH LOUD AN' CLEAR, ELLSWORTH! I'LL REEL YUH IN SLOW-LIKE!

ALL I HAVE TO DO NOW IS COME UP BY THE BOATS!

I'M BRINGIN' YUH HOME, PAL! SLOW BUT SHURE!

LET'S NOT BRAIN ME WITH THAT LIFE PRESERVER, SHALL WE?

SALUTATIONS, BOYS! I JUST SOLVED YOUR JEWEL SMUGGLING CASE TOOT SWEET!

≶HMPH!≷ THAT YUTZ COULD TANGLE HIS CORMORANT'S LINE UP WITH MINE! I'D BETTER HELP HIM!

≶OOF! URK! ACK!≷ GAWRSH...

88

...THAT THEY ARE THE JUICIEST, MOST DELECTABLE OF ALL THE *BIRDS!*

ZOO LOGIC

BIRDS!?

SEE WHAT I MEAN?

CULINARY PERSUASION! WHO WOULD HAVE THOUGHT?

LET'S GO, BOY! HEEL!

I BETTER ALERT TABBY'S *PSYCHIATRIST* TO STAND BY!

So IT'S OFF TO THE HAPPY HUNTING GROUNDS!

I JUST GO FOR THE SPORT! PERSONALLY, I DON'T LIKE DUCK!

H. C. ANDERSEN DUCK LAKE 1 MILE

GLADYS, HERE COMES THAT CRAZY HUNTER AGAIN!

Donald Duck — "SAUCE FOR THE DUCK"

LOOK, KIDS... THE *PEWTER POT!* THAT RESTAURANT HAS A THREE-STAR RATING IN EATER'S DIGEST!

*T*HERE ARE MANY POSH RESTAURANTS IN DUCKBURG, AND DONALD KNOWS THEM ALL—!

H 8011

THERE'S THE *COPPER KETTLE!* IT WON *FOUR* STARS FOR CHEF FISHMUCK'S BRINY BOUILLABAISSE!

≋SIGH!≋ THERE'S THE *SILVER SPOON,* WHERE THE ELITE EAT UNTIL THEY'RE REPLETE! FIVE STARS!

AND THERE'S THE *GOLDEN GOURD!* SEVEN STARS FOR ITS EXCLUSIVE ARRAY OF *PATE 'GATE'!* A DIFFERENT GOOSE PASTE FOR EACH DAY OF THE WEEK! SHEER CULINARY BLISS!

BUT THE *PLATINUM PAN* TOPS THEM ALL! THAT PLACE IS **THE** NEWEST AND SNOOTIEST IN TOWN! RUMOR HAS IT THEY MAKE A *WORLD-CLASS SAUCE!*

MAYBE ONE OF THESE DAYS *I'LL* BE CALLED TO THAT KITCHEN! DONALD DUCK, PURVEYOR OF PRINCELY PROVENDER AND *ARTIST* IN ANTIPASTO!

MAYBE! RIGHT NOW YOU'RE NEEDED *HERE!*

HOT DOGS! GETCHER RED HOTS HERE! MUSTARD, ONIONS AND *SAU-ER-KRAUT!*

EVERY BITE A CULINARY *DEEEE-LITE!!*

1

SO IT GOES... ALL DAY!

WEENIES! HEARTY 'N' HOT 'N' PLUMP EZ YEW PLEEZE!!

FOOEY! I'M *SICK* OF PANDERING TO THE PUBLIC PAUNCH! I DESERVE A *REAL* KITCHEN AND A CHANCE TO SHOW WHAT I CAN DO!

HEY! TAKE IT EASY!

IS *THAT* WHAT YOU CAN DO?! SOMEONE COULD *SLIP* ON THAT MUSTARDY MESS! BETTER GET A RAG AND WIPE IT UP BEFORE...

SLIP!

CRASH!

OWWW-WOOOOOOO!!

IT'S *MAI-FUT!* HE USED TO BE CHEF AT THE SEVEN HAPPY DRAGONS!

SORRY ABOUT THAT, MR. MAI! YOU ALL RIGHT?

MY CELESTIAL SAUCE! I WAS DELIVERING IT TO THE *PLATINUM PAN* AND NOW IT'S DOWN THE DRAIN!

I DON'T BELIEVE IT! *YOU* DO THE COOKING FOR THAT SNOOTY FOOD FARM?

NO... BUT I *DO* MAKE THEIR FAMOUS SAUCE! THIS BATCH WAS INTENDED FOR THE JUDGES OF THE EATER'S DIGEST!

THE *EATER'S DIGEST* JUDGES ARE IN TOWN? *WOW!*

COOL IT, UNCA DONALD! WE'VE GOT TO CALL AN *AMBU-LANCE* FOR MR. MAI!

②

OH, SO? AN EMISSARY OF MAI FUT OFFERED US FIRST CHANCE AT THE *GENUINE ARTICLE*... AND YOU *TURNED HIM AWAY*?

DOUBLE "GULP!" I DID, YOUR LORDSHIP!

NOW EVERY TWO-BIT EATERY IN TOWN HAS OUR SECRET INGREDIENT—AND OUR CUSTOMERS! *YOU'RE FIRED!*

YES, YOUR LORDSHIP!

SHORTLY...

UNCA DONALD, LOOK AT THE *ROADHOGGER TEN* PULLING UP AT THE CURB!

WELL, WELL! ABOUT TIME!

SIR! ARE YOU THE PROPRIETOR OF THIS... AH... *UNASSUMING* LITTLE ESTABLISHMENT?

THAT'S ME! DONALD DUCK, HOT DOG KING OF DUCK-BURG!

I AM *LORD RUNCIBLE*, OWNER OF THE PLATINUM PAN! I'VE HEARD OF YOU, MR. DUCK, AND OF YOUR *MASTERLY SAUCE*! WOULD YOU CONSIDER BECOMING OUR NEW CHEF DE CUISINE?

WOULD I EVER!

UNCA DONALD!

I'LL GATHER UP A FEW ODDS AND ENDS AND BE RIGHT WITH YOU! WATCH THE STAND WHILE I'M GONE, BOYS!

JUST REMEMBER, UNCA DONALD, THAT'S *MAI FUT'S* SAUCE YOU'RE TALKING ABOUT!

OF COURSE IT IS! I'M JUST *DELIVERING* IT! IF I DO MYSELF A *SMALL FAVOR* ON THE WAY, WHERE'S THE HARM IN THAT?

WHAT'S SAUCE FOR MAI FUT IS SAUCE FOR YOUR UNCLE! TOODLE-OO!

I SMELL TROUBLE BREWING, MEN! MR. MAI *TRUSTED* HIM!

IT'S NOT LIKE UNCA DONALD WAS *BREAKING ANY RULES*! BUT HE SURE DOES *BEND* THEM!

112

119

120

127

I'VE NEVER BOUGHT *ANYTHING* I COULDN'T MAKE A *PROFIT* ON AND I DON'T INTEND TO LET THIS HUNK OF ROCK SPOIL MY RECORD!

SCREECH!

Z.

THAT'S WHY I BROUGHT YOU BOYS ALONG! YOU'RE TO HELP ME SCOUT THE MOUNTAIN FOR SOMETHING *VALUABLE!*

HSSSS

SURE! WE'LL CHECK FOR MINERAL AND GEM DEPOSITS!

AAH...WHADDA' *YOU* MICROBES KNOW ABOUT ROCKS?

WE'RE FIVE-STAR C.R.A.K.E.R.J.A.C.S. IN THE JUNIOR WOODCHUCKS!

CONNOISSEUR ROCK-HOUNDS AND *ALL-KNOWING EXPERTS* IN *RECOGNIZING* JEWELS AND *ALL* CHOICE STONES!

EXCELLENT! I KNEW YOU'D BE HELPFUL!

THAT'S NOTHING! *I* WAS QUITE THE ROCK EXPERT IN MY DAY!

THE LITTLE BOONEHEADS NAMED ME CHAMPION *ROCKHOUND* AND *ADEPT* COLLECTOR OF *KEEN* PEBBLES AND OTHER *TREASURES!*

YOU WERE A C.R.A.C.K.P.O.T.?

I DON'T LIKE TO *BRAG,* BUT ⸘AHEM⸘...

I STARTED MY FORTUNE AS A PROSPECTOR, BUT THESE OLD BONES NEED A LITTLE *HELP* TO CLIMB MOUNTAINS NOWADAYS!

133

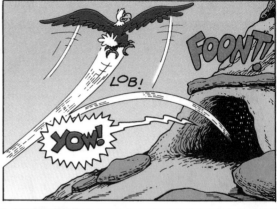

137

≹GROAN!≹ MY BACK!

WHAT ARE *YOU* SMILING ABOUT?

IMAGINE WHAT THAT DESCENT SAVED ME IN *HOURLY WAGES!*

BUT ≹SOB!≹ I OWN A WHOLE MOUNTAIN OF NOTHING BUT WORTHLESS, *FRACTURED ROCK!*

HEY, THERE!

SNEE-KAH HIGHWAY CONSTRUCTION

HOW MUCH IS YOUR *GRAVEL?* IT WILL SAVE US THE 150-MILE TRIP INTO TOWN!

SN HIGH CONST

AND SO...

YOU SEE, KIDS, *I* ALWAYS TURN A PROFIT!

IT'S A MIGHTY *SMALL* PROFIT!

McDUCK'S *GRAVEL* CO. $.50 PER LOAD NO OVERHEAD! JUST SKY!

SNEE-KAH HIGHWAY CONSTRUCTION

BUT THAT'S A MIGHTY *BIG* MOUNTAIN! BESIDES, I'M HOLDING DOWN THE *OVERHEAD!*

THE GRAVEL BIN'S GETTING LOW! TELL DONALD TO START UP THE ROCK-CRUSHER!

UNCA DONALD...

I HEARD HIM! I HEARD HIM!

ROCK CRUSHER

Walt Disney's Donald Duck in The Leaning Tower of Meatloaf

DINNER TIME AT THE DUCK HOUSE!

HUNGRY, BOYS?

I'M SO STARVED I COULD EAT A HOUSE!

I COULD EAT *TWO* HOUSES!

I COULD EAT AN ENTIRE APARTMENT BUILDING AND STILL HAVE ROOM FOR DESSERT!

D 93233

THEN GET READY FOR SOME *GOOOOOD* GRUB! MY FAMOUS MOUTH-WATERIN', RIB-STICKIN', BELLY-BUSTIN'–

MEATLOAF?! YUCK!

B-BUT YOU KIDS *ADORE* MY MEATLOAF! WHAT'S WITH THE PICKY PALATES?

WE'RE EARNING OUR NEW JUNIOR WOODCHUCK BADGES IN *GOURMET CUISINE!*

WE NOW PREFER TO *TANTALIZE* OUR TASTEBUDS...

...NOT *ANNIHILATE* THEM!

SHALL WE REPAIR TO CHEZ DUCKBURG FOR SOME *EDIBLE* EATABLES, GENTS?

INDUBITABLY!

THE NEXT MORNING!

ONLY THIS, DONALD: IT'S ALL IN THE *NAME*!

YOU'RE A COOK, JOE—WHADDAYA KNOW ABOUT *GOURMET* GRUB?

Joe's Java Joint

Fromage-Burger

Haute Dog

Pommes Frites

CREPES SUZETTE ARE JUST FANCY *FLAPJACKS*! AND *ESCARGOT*? GARDEN SLUGS!

JOE! SIX ORDER OF POMMES FRITES, THREE HAUTE DOGS, FOUR FROMAGE-BURGERS, AND A MUGGA JAVA!

SEE WHAT I MEAN?

SHUCKS, I COULD SELL *DIRTY DISHWATER* IF I CALLED IT SOMETHIN' SWANKY!

THANKS, JOE! SOUNDS MAGNIFIQUE TO THIS MAN—I MEAN, THIS *MONSIEUR*!

THAT EVENING!

I MUST ADMIT, UNCA DONALD, TONIGHT'S MENU SOUNDS *DIVINE*!

AND HOW! WHAT'S "PATÉ LE BOEUF"?

MY LATEST SPECIALTY! A TASTEBUD-TEMPTING PALATE-PLEASING, GOURMET-GRATIFYING...

...MEATLOAF? YUCK!

THE *ARROGANCE!* →SNORT!←

COME ALONG, CHAPS! LET US SEEK A MORE *REWARDING* REPAST!

CRASH!

141

142

143

...THE *LEANING TOWER OF MEATLOAF!*

GASP!!!

UH... NICE JOB, UNCA DONALD, BUT WE GOTTA GO TO *BURGERAMA* NOW!

BURGERAMA??! THAT TWO-BIT HASH HOUSE? BUT I THOUGHT YOU STUCK-UPPERS ONLY ATE *FINICKY* FOOD!

NOT ANYMORE—*NOW* WE'RE WORKING ON JUNIOR WOODCHUCK *URBAN SURVIVAL* BADGES!

AND WE HAFTA EAT *FAST FOOD* FOR FIVE DAYS STRAIGHT. IT'S A *REQUIREMENT!*

BUT BOYS! DON'T YOU WANNA EVEN *TASTE* MY TOWER OF MEATLOAF?

SORRY, UNCA DONALD! OUR *GARBAGE-BURGERS* AWAIT!

BON APPETIT!

I SAY! DO YOU KNOW WHAT THAT MEANS, GOURMANDS?

CHOW TIME FOR *US!!*

HEY! STOP, YOU VULTURES! *STOP!!*

The End!